Aberdeenshire

3111733

Drake

by C.F. Earl

Drake

by C.F. Earl

Mason Crest

Drake

Mason Crest
370 Reed Road
Broomall, Pennsylvania 19008
www.masoncrest.com

Printed and bound in the United States of America.

First printing
9 8 7 6 5 4 3 2 1

Library of Congress Cataloging-in-Publication Data

Earl, C. F.
  Drake / by C.F. Earl.
     p. cm. – (Superstars of hip-hop)
  Includes index.
  ISBN 978-1-4222-2516-5 (hardcover) – ISBN 978-1-4222-2508-0 (series hardcover) – ISBN 978-1-4222-2542-4 (softcover) – ISBN 978-1-4222-9218-1 (ebook)
  1. Drake, 1986–-Juvenile literature. 2. Rap musicians–United States–Juvenile literature. I. Title.
  ML3930.D73E27 2012
  782.421649092–dc22
  [B]
                    2011005799

Produced by Harding House Publishing Services, Inc.
www.hardinghousepages.com
Interior Design by MK Bassett-Harvey.
Cover design by Torque Advertising & Design.

Publisher's notes:
• All quotations in this book come from original sources and contain the spelling and grammatical inconsistencies of the original text.
• The Web sites mentioned in this book were active at the time of publication. The publisher is not responsible for Web sites that have changed their addresses or discontinued operation since the date of publication. The publisher will review and update the Web site addresses each time the book is reprinted.

DISCLAIMER: The following story has been thoroughly researched, and to the best of our knowledge, represents a true story. While every possible effort has been made to ensure accuracy, the publisher will not assume liability for damages caused by inaccuracies in the data, and makes no warranty on the accuracy of the information contained herein. This story has not been authorized nor endorsed by Drake.

Contents

Drive one

Hip-Hop lingo

Rap is a kind of music where rhymes are chanted, often with music in the background. When people rap, they make up these rhymes, sometimes off the top of their heads.

An **audition** is when you try out for an acting role.

Chapter 1

Drake's Start

Drake is one of **rap**'s most successful new stars. By mixing rapping and singing, Drake has found fans all over the world. His music is played on the radio and in clubs. He's only been rapping for a few years. But already, Drake's worked with some of the biggest names in music.

Drake has taken the rap world by storm. Many fans think he came up overnight. But Drake worked for years to get where he is now.

Early Life

Aubrey Drake Graham was born on October 24, 1986. His parents, Sandi and Dennis, lived in Toronto, Canada. Sandi and Dennis were very different from each other. Sandi was white, Jewish, and Canadian. Dennis was black, Catholic, and an American from Memphis, Tennessee.

Sandi was a teacher in Toronto. Dennis was a drummer. He played with Jerry Lee Lewis, a famous rock-and-roll musician.

Dennis wasn't the only musician in the family. Aubrey's uncle, Larry Graham, played bass in a group called Sly and the Family Stone. He also played with Prince. Another uncle, Teenie Hodges, wrote songs with singer Al Green.

When Aubrey was five years old, his parents split up. His father went back to Memphis. Aubrey and his mom stayed in Toronto.

Drake comes from a musical family. His uncle played bass with singer Prince and his father played drums with Jerry Lee Lewis. It's no wonder Drake was drawn to music from an early age!

Aubrey grew up mostly in Forest Hill, a suburb outside Toronto. He lived with his mother and went to school in the city. During the summers, Aubrey went to Memphis to live with his father.

Aubrey's young life was tough sometimes. After his parents split up, Aubrey had to travel a lot during the year. Sometimes he lived with his mom, sometimes with his dad. Memphis was very different from Toronto. Sometimes, Aubrey felt like he didn't fit in either place.

At school in Toronto, Aubrey felt like he didn't belong. Most kids in his school were white. Aubrey felt like they treated him differently because he was partly black and because his parents lived so far apart. He had a hard time fitting in when he went to Memphis, too. Aubrey said later that even though it was hard being different from others, it made him stronger.

Aubrey went to Forest Hill Collegiate Institute (FCHI) for high school in Toronto. While he was going to school at FCHI, Aubrey started acting.

The father of a kid in Aubrey's class worked as an agent for actors. An actor's agent helps him get acting jobs. He told his son, Aubrey's classmate, to watch for anyone who made him laugh. He wanted to talk to any kids in the high school who might have a talent for acting.

Soon, he came to talk to Aubrey. He saw Aubrey had acting skills. So he became Aubrey's agent. He helped Aubrey start his acting life.

Aubrey Breaks Into Acting

Aubrey began going to more and more **auditions**. Soon he started acting in commercials. He worked on commercials for Sears and General Motors.

When Aubrey was thirteen, a new chance came his way. In the 1980s, Linda Schuyler created the popular Canadian TV shows

Degrassi Junior High and *Degrassi High*. The shows were very popular with teens and young adults. In 2000, Linda wanted to start a new show. She thought another *Degrassi* show could be popular with fans who hadn't seen the shows in the '80s. The new show was named *Degrassi: The Next Generation*.

Schuyler and the new show's other creators started looking for a group of young actors. They wanted to find students that teenagers could relate to. They also wanted to find actors who were the same age as the characters on the show. Other shows at the time were using actors much older than their characters. The creators of *Degrassi* wanted their show to be different.

Six hundred Canadian students auditioned for *Degrassi: The Next Generation*. Aubrey was one of that group. Out of all of those young actors, Aubrey got a part on the new show. He was chosen to play a high school student named Jimmy Brooks.

The first episode of *Degrassi: The Next Generation* was shown on October 14, 2001. The show was on one of Canada's biggest TV channels, CTV. The first season of *Degrassi* had more than 350,000 young Canadians watching every week. The show was a huge hit. Aubrey turned fourteen a little more than a week after the first episode was shown. Even though he was young, he was already doing things most other young people could only dream about.

Over the next few years, *Degrassi* would become an even bigger success. Soon it was shown in the United States, too. The show gained more and more fans. Many young people just couldn't get enough *Degrassi*. Soon, the actors on the show were stars.

While working on *Degrassi*, Aubrey was also doing other acting. He had small parts in a few TV shows. In 2002, Aubrey had a part in a TV movie called *Conviction*. The movie starred actor Omar Epps. Still, *Degrassi* was Aubrey's main acting work. Playing Jimmy Brooks was a full-time job for the young actor.

Drake grew up in Toronto, Canada. He says that the city has been a big part of his musical life.

Drake went to high school at the Forest Hill Collegiate Institute in Toronto. He never finished high school, though. Instead, he left school early to follow his dreams of acting.

Aubrey was still a teenager, but he was already famous in Canada. Aubrey never graduated from high school, though. He ended up leaving school before he could get his diploma. Instead, he started to focus on acting. *Degrassi* helped make him a star. Over the next few years, he worked hard to give *Degrassi* his all. Aubrey wanted to do the best job he could at whatever he was doing. And soon, he wouldn't be just working on his acting.

Hip-Hop lingo

When you **record** music, you perform and save the performance on a computer or a CD.

A **mixtape** is a collection of a few songs put on a CD or given away for free on the Internet without being professionally recorded.

Producers are the people in charge of putting together songs. A producer makes the big decisions about the music.

An **album** is a group of songs collected together on a CD.

Remixes are new versions of songs that have already been on an earlier CD or have been done by another artist.

A **single** is a song that is sold by itself.

A **music video** is a short film of a song's performance.

A **contract** is a written agreement between two people. Once you've signed a contract, it's against the law to break it. When a musician signs a contract with a music company, the musician promises to give all her music to that company for them to produce as CDs and then sell—and the music company promises to pay the musician a certain amount of money. Usually, a contract is for a certain period of time.

A **record label** is a company that produces music for singers and groups and puts out CDs.

A **studio** is a place where musicians go to record their music and turn it into CDs.

Chapter 2

Aubrey Becomes Drake

By 2006, Aubrey had been acting for a few years. He had been successful in *Degrassi: The Next Generation*. He had fans across Canada. The actors from *Degrassi* traveled around the country. They went to malls all over Canada to visit their fans. Wherever the young actors went, thousands of fans came to see them. Many fans came just to see Aubrey. Even though he was still very young, Aubrey had done a lot in just a few years.

Aubrey loved acting, but he also loved music. He'd grown up in a musical family. Music had always been a big part of his life. Now, Aubrey started working on his own music.

Aubrey decided to use his middle name, Drake, for rap. He'd go by Aubrey Graham on *Degrassi* and **record** music as Drake. Drake spent some of the money he'd made acting to start recording some songs. Soon, he had the chance to work on his first **mixtape**.

Room for Improvement

In 2006, Drake released his first mixtape. He called it *Room for Improvement*.

With *Comeback Season*, Drake had more people listening to his music than ever before. He also worked with some famous artists for the mixtape.

Drake recorded the mixtape with DJ Smallz. Smallz was known for his Southern Smoke series of mixtapes. He'd recorded mixtapes with Lil Wayne, Young Jeezy, and other artists. Drake also had help on *Room for Improvement* from **producers** Boi-1da and Noah "40" Shebib.

Room for Improvement had 23 songs on it. Most were Drake's own songs. Three songs from the **album** were **remixes** of other artists' songs. Drake remixed Trey Songz's "About the Game" and rapper Lupe Fiasco's "Kick, Push." *Room for Improvement* also featured rapper Nickelus F. and Canadian singer Voyce.

At first, Drake wanted to sell the mixtape. But it only sold a few thousand copies. So, Drake decided to put the tape out for free. Soon, people were downloading *Room for Improvement* over the Internet. By putting the mixtape online, Drake could get more people to hear it.

It wasn't long before Drake was back to recording music. He wanted to do everything he could to make it big in music.

Comeback Season

In 2007, Drake put out his second mixtape. It was called *Comeback Season.*

Comeback Season had 24 songs on it. Drake worked with more guest artists than he had on *Room for Improvement.* He worked on a song with R&B singer Robin Thicke. He also worked with the rap group Little Brother. Drake rapped with fellow Canadian MC Kardinal Offishall. Drake also remixed a song from rappers Brisco and Flo Rida called "Man of the Year." The song featured Lil Wayne. Drake kept the Lil Wayne part of the song and rapped his own verses over it.

Singer Trey Songz helped Drake on four songs. He had heard some of Drake's music before *Comeback Season.* He thought Drake could be the next big thing in rap. Trey wanted to do what he could to help Drake make it. He was a popular singer. He knew his voice on a Drake song would get the Canadian rapper some new listeners.

Trey Songz was right. Drake put out a **single** the two had done together. The song was called "Replacement Girl." Drake even made a **music video** for the song. The video was played on BET in

Singer Trey Songz helped Drake on his mixtape *Comeback Season*. He helped to take Drake's musical career to the next level.

the United States. It was shown as the "New Joint of the Day" on the TV show *106 & Park* in April 2007. People were starting to pay attention to Drake's music.

On both his mixtapes, Drake recorded with Boi-1da and Noah "40" Shebib. 40 had been recording songs with Drake since 2005. Drake and 40 were both young actors who loved rap. They got along really well.

With two mixtapes out, Drake was working his way into the music world. He was gaining more fans all the time. And it wouldn't be long before Drake had a new fan at the very top of the rap game.

Meeting Lil Wayne

Soon, Drake got a huge break. Jas Prince, the son of the head of Rap-A-Lot Records, was searching for new artists on MySpace.com. He found Drake's page and listened to "Replacement Girl." Jas was surprised to find Drake hadn't signed a **contract** with a **record label.** He had a music video for "Replacement Girl" and the song featured the popular singer Trey Songz. But he didn't have a deal with a record company.

Jas emailed Drake. He wanted to find out if Drake really was on a label. Drake e-mailed back to say he wasn't. After that, the two talked more. They became friends. Jas thought Drake could be the next big thing in hip-hop. He could rap, sing, and act. Jas thought Drake could be a star.

Jas wanted to help find Drake a record label. He gave Drake's music to his friends and told them to listen to the new artist. One of Jas's friends was rapper Lil Wayne. Jas told Wayne about Drake's music. But at first, Wayne didn't really listen.

At the end of 2007, Jas was performing with Lil Wayne. It was a New Year's Eve concert in Houston, Texas, Jas's hometown. The day after the concert, Jas went for a drive with Wayne. While they were in the car, Jas put on Drake's music.

Lil Wayne listened for a minute and then asked who the rapper was. Jas told Wayne it was the same artist he'd been talking about. Next, Jas played a Drake song called "Brand New" for Wayne. Wayne asked Jas who the singer was. Jas told Wayne Drake could also sing. Wayne couldn't believe it. Drake could rap and sing well, and he was an actor, too. He realized Jas might be right. Drake just might be the next big name in hip-hop. Wayne told Jas to call Drake right away. Wayne wanted to meet the new Canadian artist.

Jas called Drake. Then, he handed the phone to Wayne. When Drake answered his phone, he expected to hear Jas's voice. "Yo, it's Weezy," Wayne said.

Drake was shocked. He couldn't believe Lil Wayne was really on the phone. Wayne told Drake to get on the next flight to Houston. Drake said he would. He wasn't about to miss this chance. The next day, Drake was on a plane from Toronto to Texas.

Joining Young Money

The first night Drake was in Houston, he and Lil Wayne went to the recording **studio**. They started working on some new music together, getting to know each other. The next day, Jas, Drake, and Wayne drove from Houston to Atlanta, Georgia, in Lil Wayne's tour bus. When they got there, they went to the studio again. That night, Drake and Wayne recorded the first version of "Forever." The song would go on to be a big hit for both artists. They worked on a few more songs together, too.

Drake and Lil Wayne got along well. They also found they worked well together on music. Wayne saw Drake had lots of talent. He knew a rapper who could also sing could be a successful artist.

Drake's life had suddenly changed. He'd been living and working in Toronto. Now, he was in the United States, rhyming alongside one of rap's biggest stars. In 2008, Wayne sold a million copies of his album *Tha Carter III* in one week! For Drake, this was a huge step toward his dream.

Lil Wayne had a record label called Young Money Entertainment. He didn't sign Drake right away, though. Drake and Lil Wayne became good friends. But Drake was still making his way in music without a label.

Drake was so close to making it big in the music world. He didn't have a record deal, but, so far, he hadn't needed one. He'd become successful on his own. Putting out his own music over the Internet was a great way for Drake to reach lots of people. With the Internet, Drake didn't need a big company to get people to hear his music.

Hip-Hop lingo

The **beat** is the basic rhythm or pulse of a piece of music.

The **singles chart** is a list of the best-selling songs for a week.

R&B stands for "rhythm and blues." It's a kind of music that African Americans made popular in the 1940s. It has a very strong beat. Today, it's a style of music that's a lot like hip-hop.

Pop is short for "popular." Pop music is usually light and happy, with a good beat.

A **soundtrack** is a collection of all the songs on a movie.

Chapter 3

A Rising Star

Drake had two mixtapes out, and both had done well. He was starting to make his mark on the music world. More and more people were hearing his songs. But Drake was still an actor first and a rapper second. Soon, that would all change.

Leaving Degrassi

In 2008, Drake left *Degrassi*. The show's producers planned to bring in a new cast. They wanted younger actors to play a new class of high school kids. Drake was also working hard on his music. It was tough to leave the show he'd been on for years. Drake knew it was the right thing to do, though.

In Canada, Drake was famous for playing his character on *Degrassi*. He'd gained lots of success thanks to the show. But now, it was time to move on. Drake's last episode aired on August 15, 2008. He'd been in more than 100 episodes of the show.

Now, he could put all his energy into his music. He used the money he'd made on *Degrassi* to record as much as he could. He worked hard

Lil Wayne heard Drake's music and knew that the Canadian rapper could be a big star. Wayne made sure he worked with Drake right away.

on a third mixtape. His music was becoming more and more popular. He had to make sure the new mixtape was his best so far. He needed to show people he was worth their attention.

So Far Gone—The Mixtape

Drake released his third mixtape, *So Far Gone*, on February 13, 2009. Drake put out the mixtape for free on his website. To celebrate its release, Drake held a party in Toronto. The party was at a club called 6 Degrees. Basketball player Lebron James even showed up.

For *So Far Gone*, Drake recorded with some big artists and producers. Drake's new friend Lil Wayne rapped on four songs. Drake also worked with rappers Lloyd and Bun-B. Singers Omarion and Santigold also recorded songs with Drake for *So Far Gone*. Kanye West made the beat for a song called "Say What's Real." Producer Just Blaze worked on the **beat** for a song with Drake and Lil Wayne.

The *So Far Gone* mixtape had two singles on it. The first was called "Best I Ever Had." Drake's friend Boi-1da produced the song. The second single was called "Successful." "Successful" featured Drake's friends Trey Songz and Lil Wayne.

"Best I Ever Had" was a big hit. The song reached number two on the Hot 100 **singles chart**. It made it to the very top of the rap and **R&B** charts. It even went to number ten on the **pop** singles chart. In June 2009, Drake put out the music video for the song. Kanye West worked on the video with Drake.

"Successful" did very well, too. It reached number three on the R&B singles chart. It also made it to number two on the rap singles chart. Drake's friend 40 made the beat for "Successful." 40 helped on every song for *So Far Gone*. He made sure all the songs sounded the way Drake wanted.

So Far Gone helped Drake's music reach new heights. The tape's singles were hits. They helped more people hear Drake's music. With "Best I Ever Had" on radio and TV, Drake was gaining lots of new fans.

With the release of *So Far Gone*, Drake had more fans than ever. Drake was ready to give fans more music after signing to Young Money, too.

Signing to Young Money

Drake was friends with Lil Wayne. He'd been on tour with him. But up to that point, he still hadn't signed a contract with his company. Drake had done what very few artists can. He'd reached success without a record company's help.

By using the Internet to get his music out, Drake had become popular before getting signed to a label. Most artists don't reach the same level of success until after they have help from a record company. Record labels help get an artist's music in stores. They also help spread the word about a new artist.

Instead of taking that path, Drake put his music out for free online. He wanted to get as many people to hear him as possible. Then, in 2009, he finally signed to Young Money, after doing well on his own. He had lots of people talking about him. His songs were becoming more and more popular. Many thought Drake might become the next big success in hip-hop.

Drake's Big Year

In August 2009, Drake's song "Forever" was released on the **soundtrack** of a movie about Lebron James. The movie was called *More Than a Game.*

"Forever" was first recorded with Lil Wayne when he and Drake went to Atlanta. The *More Than a Game* soundtrack had a different recording of the song. The new recording featured rappers Kanye West and Eminem, as well as Drake and Lil Wayne. Drake was rapping on the same track as some of the biggest names in hip-hop.

"Forever" was a huge hit. It reached number eight on the Hot 100 singles chart. It made it to number one on the R&B and rap singles charts.

On September 15, 2009, Young Money put out a shorter version of *So Far Gone.* The new *So Far Gone* only had seven songs on it.

The short album had some songs from the mixtape version of *So Far Gone*. Two of the album's songs were new. One of the new songs was also released as a single. It was called "I'm Goin In." Lil Wayne rapped on it with Drake.

The shorter *So Far Gone* was a huge hit. In its first week out, the album sold 73,000 copies. It was also number six on the album charts that week. In 2009, *So Far Gone* was the seventh best-selling rap album. By the end of the next year, *So Far Gone* had sold more than 500,000 copies. The album was a success as both a mixtape and then as a short album.

Drake also worked with some of the biggest artists in the world in 2009. He recorded a song called "The One" with Mary J. Blige. The song was on Mary's album *Stronger with Each Tear*. He rapped on the remix to singer/actor Jamie Foxx's song "Digital Girl." The remix also featured Kanye West and singer The-Dream. He was also featured on "Say Something" by Timbaland. The song was very popular. It reached number one on the R&B and rap singles charts.

Rapper Birdman's album *Pricele$$* featured Drake on two songs, as well. The songs were called "Money to Blow" and "4 My Town (Play Ball)." Lil Wayne also rapped on both the songs. Birdman ran Cash Money Records. Cash Money owned Young Money. Birdman and Lil Wayne were very close. The two rappers often talked about how they were like father and son. "Money to Blow" turned out to be a big hit. The song reached number two on both the R&B and rap singles charts.

Drake was also a big part of *We Are Young Money*. The album was meant to show off Lil Wayne's new Young Money rappers. Drake was on five songs from the album. *We Are Young Money* reached the top of the rap albums chart.

Not many new rappers get to work with superstars like Kanye West, but Drake was already on his way to becoming a star himself with the release of "Forever" and *So Far Gone*.

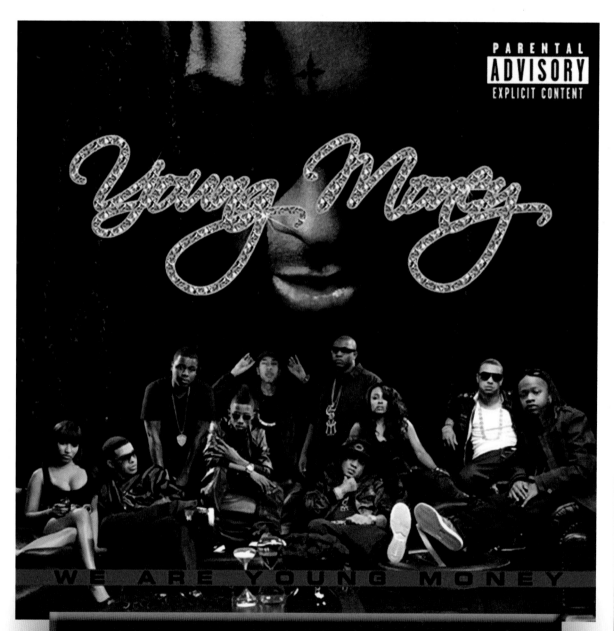

We Are Young Money allowed Lil Wayne to show off all of the rappers on his label. Drake and Nicki Minaj both appear on the album. Soon, the two would be the biggest stars on Young Money.

That year, 2009, was a huge one for Drake. "Best I Ever Had" and "Forever" had been big hits. His mixtapes had helped him find rap success. Now, Drake's fans wanted to know what he'd do for his first full album.

It wouldn't be long before they'd find out. Nothing was going to stop Drake from making it to the top of the rap world.

Hip-Hop lingo

Each year, the National Academy of Recording Arts and Sciences gives out the Grammy Awards (short for Gramophone Awards)—or **Grammys**—to people who have done something really big in the music industry. When someone has been **nominated**, he has been picked as one of the people who might win an award.

Chapter 4

Drake Makes It Big

After *So Far Gone*, Drake was on his way to being a star. At the 2010 **Grammys**, Drake even performed "Forever" with Lil Wayne, Eminem, and drummer/producer Travis Barker. Drake didn't even have a full album out. But he was already at the Grammys. His song "Best I Ever Had" was **nominated** for two Grammys.

Many people saw Drake as the next big artist in hip-hop. He had Lil Wayne and Young Money behind him. His mixtapes had brought him lots of attention and success. Now, he had to prove he could put out a great album.

The pressure was on for Drake. But he knew he was up to it. He put all his energy into making his first album the best it could be.

Thank Me Later

Drake put out his first full album on June 15, 2010. It was called *Thank Me Later*.

Drake worked with many of music's biggest artists for *Thank Me Later*. T.I., Alicia Keys, Jay-Z, Young Jeezy, and The-Dream all helped Drake on songs for the album. Nicki Minaj also worked with Drake on a song. Nicki and Drake had been friends since she joined Young Money. She and Drake had worked together on songs for the *We Are Young Money* album. For *Thank Me Later*, Nicki rapped on a song called "Up All Night."

Like Drake, Nicki Minaj has become one of the biggest stars in rap. The two Young Money rappers have worked together on more than one song. There are even rumors that the two might have dated.

Noah "40" Shebib and Boi-1da both worked on *Thank Me Later*, too. They'd helped Drake on all his mixtapes. Drake worked well with both producers, so he knew he wanted their help on his first album. Drake also had beats from Kanye West and Timbaland on the album. Kanye made the beat for "Find Your Love" and "Show Me a Good Time. Timbaland worked on "Thank Me Now."

Drake put out four singles from *Thank Me Later*. The first was called "Over." It was a huge hit for Drake. The song made it to number 14 on the Hot 100 singles chart. It reached number two on the R&B singles chart. And it hit number one on the rap singles chart.

The next single was called "Find Your Love." Drake didn't rap at all on the song. Instead, he sang the whole thing. Drake worked with Kanye West on it. The song was an even bigger hit than "Over." It reached number five on the Hot 100 singles chart.

"Miss Me" was the third single. Drake rapped the verses and sang the chorus. Lil Wayne rapped a verse, too.

The last single from *Thank Me Later* was called "Fancy." The song featured T.I. and producer Swizz Beatz, who also made the beat for the single. Both "Miss Me" and "Fancy" did very well. They were both near the top of the Hot 100, R&B, and rap singles charts.

Thank Me Later was a huge success. In its first week out, the album sold 447,000 copies. It hit number one on the album charts in the same week. The rapper from Toronto, Canada, now had the number-one album in the United States.

Just over one month after *Thank Me Later* came out, it had sold more than a million copies. By the end of 2010, the album had sold more than 1,279,000 copies. Drake had become one of music's biggest new stars.

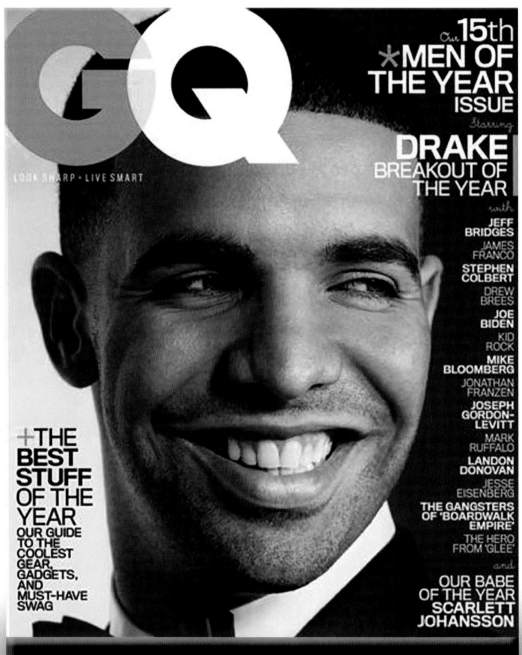

Drake had every reason to smile at the end of 2010. He'd become music's newest star with the success of his first album, *Thank Me Later*. And he was just getting started.

The 2011 Grammy Awards

In February 2011, Drake went to the 53rd Grammy Awards. Drake took his mother to the award show. She had always supported Drake. She was there for him while he was on *Degrassi* and when he moved into music.

Drake was nominated for four awards. "Over" was nominated for Best Rap Solo Performance. "Fancy" was up for Best Rap Performance by a Duo or Group. *Thank Me Later* was nominated for Best Rap Album.

Drake was up against many of rap's biggest artists for the Best Rap Album award. Eminem's *Recovery* was nominated for the award. Jay-Z's *Blueprint 3* was, too. Drake was new in the world of hip-hop. But he was already nominated for the same award as two of the biggest hip-hop artists of all time.

Drake was also up for the Best New Artist award. With the other nominations, Drake was going against other rappers. For the Best New Artist award, Drake was up against artists performing many different styles of music. He was up against singer Justin Bieber and British band Florence & the Machine. He wasn't just out for himself, though. He was hip-hop's chance at the Best New Artist award for 2011.

With *Thank Me Later*, Drake had toured the world and had hit songs. His first album was a success. He'd reached his dreams of making it in music. But Drake wasn't about to slow down now that he was successful. He was already working on his next album. Drake wanted to give his fans an even better album with his second.

Take Care

In December 2010, *GQ* magazine put out an issue listing their Men of the Year. The magazine named Drake Breakout of the Year. In an interview for the issue, Drake had some special news for fans.

He told the interviewer he was planning to call his new album *Take Care.*

The special issue of GQ was the first time fans had heard what Drake was working on after *Thank Me Later*. In the GQ interview, Drake didn't say much more about the album than its name. But he did talk about a few of the producers he was working with.

Drake talked about working with his friend Noah "40" Shebib. 40 had worked on *Thank Me Later*. The producer had been working with Drake since he was on *Degrassi*. Drake also said he was working with his friend Boi-1da. He and Drake had been working together for a long time, too. Boi-1da made the beat for "Forever" and for Drake's first single, "Replacement Girl."

In an interview with MTV, Boi-1da talked about working with Drake on *Take Care*. The producer said Drake really wanted to prove he was a great rapper. With the new album, Drake wanted to show people he could be more than a singing rapper. Not everyone liked Drake singing so much on *Thank Me Later*. Drake was ready to help those fans remember why they first fell in love with his music. With *Take Care*, Boi-1da said Drake wanted to make sure people knew he was a rapper first and a singer second.

Drake also talked to interviewers about focusing on rapping for his second album. "*Take Care* is its own mission," he told interviewers on the hip-hop radio station Shade 45. "I've never had this many raps," he said.

In January 2011, Drake talked to the UK's DJ Semtex about *Take Care*. He told Semtex he didn't like how quickly he had to finish *Thank Me Later*. He said that's why he named his next album *Take Care*. Drake wanted to make sure he took his time with his second album. He wanted to make sure it was something really special.

Drake worked hard on his second album. And his fans couldn't have been more excited when *Take Care* was released at the end of

The cover of Drake's second album, *Take Care*, fit with the ideas on the album. Drake may have become rich and successful, but that doesn't mean his life is perfect. Drake often raps about the downside of success.

2011. Drake's hard work paid off for the Canadian rapper. The album was a huge hit with fans and critics. *Take Care* was the best-selling album in the United States in its first week out. The album sold more than 600,000 copies that week! *Take Care* was a hit in Canada and the UK, too.

Drake worked with many big stars on *Take Care*. He recorded songs with Lil Wayne, Nicki Minaj, Rick Ross, and Rihanna. Drake also worked with new artists like singer The Weeknd and rapper Kendrick Lamar. The Weeknd is also from Drake's hometown of Toronto and helped Drake with a few songs. Superstar singer Stevie Wonder even helped Drake with *Take Care*!

The first single from *Take Care* was called "Headlines." The song was released in the summer before Take Care came out. In October, Drake put out the next single, a song with Nicki Minaj called "Make Me Proud." Drake put out a song with Lil Wayne called "The Motto" as *Take Care*'s third single.

Drake put out "Take Care" as the album's fourth single. Rihanna sang the song's hook. Drake put out a video for the song that also featured Rihanna. After working together to create a hit for Rihanna with her song "What's My Name?," Rihanna was able to work with Drake to make another big song for his album. "Take Care" was a hit in the United States and in the UK.

Many critics named *Take Care* one of the best albums of 2011. Just a few months after its release, Drake had sold more than one and a half million copies of *Take Care*. Drake went from giving away mixtapes online to selling more than a million copies of his album!

Looking to the Future

Drake had come a long way from being a Canadian teen actor. In just a few short years, he went from actor to rapper. Today, he's become one of the biggest names in music.

Few new artists reach the heights Drake has. Fans and critics loved his first and second albums. He has fans around the world. Many of rap's most famous stars say they like his music.

He may be new to the music world, but Drake's always known what he wanted. Since he was just thirteen, Drake's worked hard to make his dreams come true. Drake's future is wide open, too. He's talked about working in more movies and making more music. The rapper has shown he's able to do lots of different things, from rapping to singing to acting. Drake's fans are waiting to hear—or watch—whatever he puts out next.

1986   Aubrey Drake Graham (or "Drake") is born on October 24, 1986 in Toronto, Canada.

1991   At the age of five, Drake's parents divorce.

2001   Drake begins his acting career. He plays the role of Jimmy Brooks on the show *Degrassi: The Next Generation.*

2006   Drake releases a mixtape called *Room for Improvement* on his website and MySpace page.

2007   Drake releases another mixtape, called *Comeback Season.*

    His second mixtape carries the single "Replacement Girl."

    In April, Drake becomes the first unsigned Canadian artist to appear on BET when BET plays the music video for "Replacement Girl."

2008   Lil Wayne hears Drake's music. He invites Drake to fly to Houston and tour with him. While on tour, the duo record "Ransom," "I Want This Forever," and "Brand New" together.

2009   Drake's first two hit singles, "Best I Ever Had" and "Ever Girl," go to the top ten of the charts.

    On June 29, Drake signs a record deal with Lil Wayne's label, Young Money Entertainment.

    Drake's third mixtape, called *So Far Gone*, sells over 500,000 copies in the U.S.

Time Line

2010   In March, Drake releases the single "Over."

Drake sings on a song for the group Young Artists for Haiti.

On June 15, Drake's first official album is released, called *Thank Me Later.* The album goes on to sell 447,000 records in its first week, setting the record for 2010.

In November, Drake says that his second album will be called *Take Care.*

2011   Drake releases *Take Care.*

In Books

Baker, Soren. *The History of Rap and Hip Hop*. San Diego, Calif.: Lucent, 2006.

Comissiong, Solomon W. F. *How Jamal Discovered Hip-Hop Culture*. New York: Xlibris, 2008.

Cornish, Melanie. *The History of Hip Hop*. New York: Crabtree, 2009.

Czekaj, Jef. *Hip and Hop, Don't Stop!* New York: Hyperion, 2010.

Haskins, Jim. *One Nation Under a Groove: Rap Music and Its Roots*. New York: Jump at the Sun, 2000.

Hatch, Thomas. *A History of Hip-Hop: The Roots of Rap*. Portsmouth, N.H.: Red Bricklearning, 2005.

Websites

Cash Money Records Website
www.cashmoney-records.com

Degrassi TV Show
www.teennick.com/shows/degrassi

Drake Fansite
drizzydrakemusic.com

Drake on Myspace
www.myspace.com/drake

The Official Drake Website
www.drakeofficial.com

Discography
Albums

2009	So Far Gone (EP)
2010	Thank Me Later
2011	Take Care

Index

Index

About the Author

C.F. Earl is a writer living and working in Binghamton, New York. Earl writes mostly on social and historical topics, including health, the military, and finances. An avid student of the world around him, and particularly fascinated with almost any current issue, C.F. Earl hopes to continue to write for books, websites, and other publications for as long as he is able.

Picture Credits

Benson Kua: p. 11
Carrienelson1, Dreamstime.com: pp. 6, 18, 22, 34
Featureflash, Dreamstime.com: p. 24
GQ Magazine: p. 36
Karla Moy - hustlegrl.com: p. 26
Laurence Agron, Dreamstime.com: p. 29
OVO: p. 16
Sbukley, Dreamstime.com: p. 1
Simon Wedege Petersen, Dreamstime.com: 8
SimonP: p. 12
thecomeupshow: pp. 14, 32
Universal/Cash Money: p. 39
Young Money Entertainment: p. 30

To the best knowledge of the publisher, all other images are in the public domain. If any image has been inadvertently uncredited, please notify Harding House Publishing Services, Vestal, New York 13850, so that rectification can be made for future printings.